AF228850

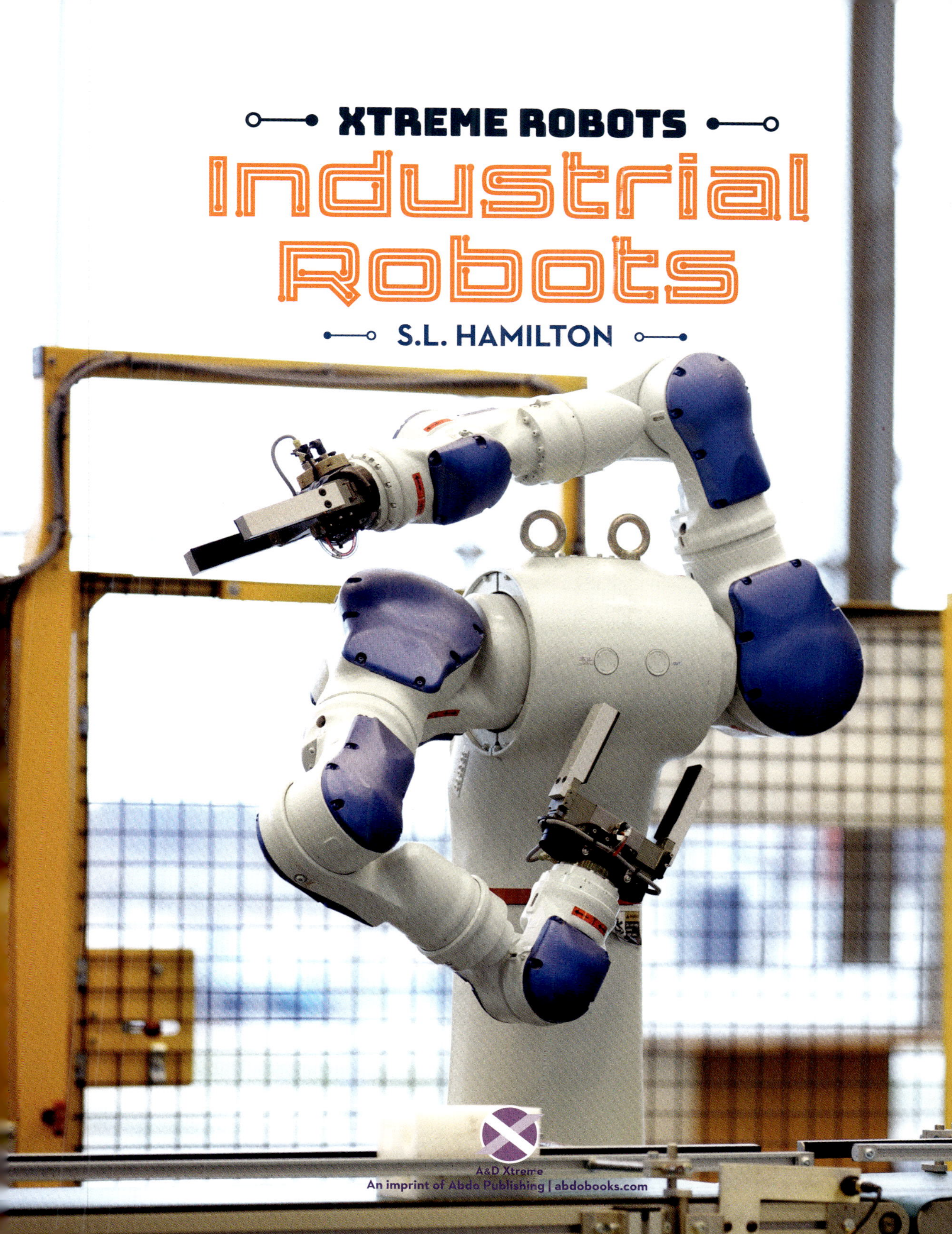

XTREME ROBOTS
Industrial Robots
S.L. HAMILTON
A&D Xtreme
An imprint of Abdo Publishing | abdobooks.com

Printed in the United States of America, North Mankato, MN.
112018
012019

Editor: John Hamilton
Copy Editor: Bridget O'Brien
Graphic Design: Sue Hamilton
Cover Design: Candice Keimig and Pakou Moua
Cover Photo: Science Source
Interior Photos & Illustrations: ABB Group-pgs 6-7;
Adidas-pgs 12 & 13; Alabama Department of Commerce-pg 1;
Alamy-pgs 21 (bottom) & 22-23; Boeing-pgs 10-11;
Boston Dynamics-pg 25; Creator Restaurant-pgs 16 & 17;
Festo-pgs 2-3; Intuitive Surgical-pgs 26-27; iStock-pg 20 (Lego Robot);
Rethink Robotics/HAHN Group-pgs 28, 29 & 32;
Science Source-pgs 20 (top), 21 (top) & 24;
Shutterstock-pgs 4-5, 8-9, 20 (Lego blocks bottom) & 30-31;
Unifiller Systems-pgs 14 & 15; Zume Pizza-pgs 18 & 19.

Library of Congress Control Number: 2018950003
Publisher's Cataloging-in-Publication Data

Names: Hamilton, S.L., author.
Title: Industrial robots / by S.L. Hamilton.
Description: Minneapolis, Minnesota : Abdo Publishing, 2019 |
Series: Xtreme robots | Includes online resources and index.
Identifiers: ISBN 9781532118265 (lib. bdg.) |
    ISBN 9781532171444 (ebook)
Subjects: LCSH: Robots, Industrial--Juvenile literature. |
    Robots--Juvenile literature. | Computer integrated
    manufacturing systems--Juvenile literature. |
    Robotics--Juvenile literature.
Classification: DDC 629.892--dc23

Contents

Industrial Robots

Industrial robots are workers. Some do jobs that require a high level of care and precision, such as assembly, welding, and painting. Others load, unload, and move heavy boxes. Some are used for packaging, labeling, and shipping. From car manufacturing to cake decorating, engineers and programmers create robots to work and assist humans in thousands of different industries.

Assembly Robots

Robots build many different products. They protect humans from heavy lifting, dangerous materials, and tasks that are done over and over. The automobile industry has used mechanical workers for decades. Robots do many jobs in car and motorcycle production. Welding robots send sparks flying in automobile assembly lines. These robots heat car body panels to the melting point and join them together. This hot and sometimes dangerous work needs to be perfect every time. Some robots have precision jobs, such as placing small parts on engines. Others move heavy car parts for assembly. Glass windshields and tires are also placed on cars by robots.

Robots are programmed to follow a specific path of action. This allows them to spray car parts and other products with even, clean coats of paint.

Spraying robots use paint, sealers, primers, and adhesives. These liquids are toxic to humans. The robots' work means humans are not exposed to dangerous chemicals.

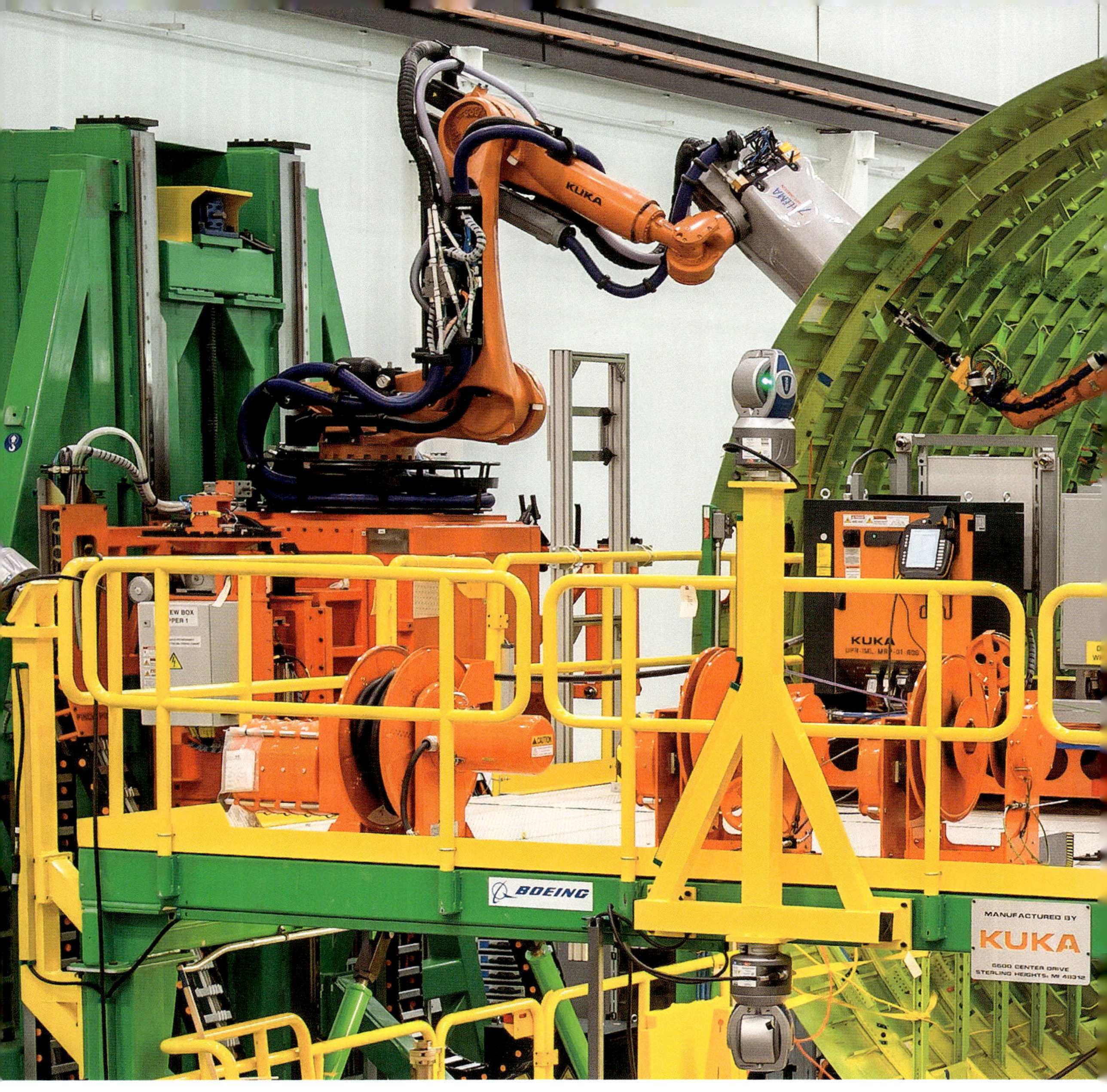

The Boeing company uses robots to place the 60,000 rivets that hold a Boeing 777 jet together. Human operators position the plane's panels. Robots called FAUB (Fuselage Automated Upright Build) roll into place inside the plane.

FAUB (pronounced "fob") robots drill holes and insert rivets. This kind of repetitive work has caused injuries to human arms, shoulders, and backs. Robots can be placed in the awkward positions required to get the job done.

Shoe-Making Robots

Adidas uses robots in a "Speedfactory" to create new running shoes. Since shoe designs change all the time, Adidas turned to robots to help them make fewer numbers of certain shoes. Instead of making 50,000 to 100,000 pairs of shoes, as is done in an Adidas factory, the Speedfactory robots can be programmed to build as few as 500 pairs. If the shoe is redesigned, the program can be changed quickly. The robots begin making new shoe designs in as little as a few weeks.

An Adidas Speedfactory robot with a completed running shoe. Adidas produces up to 600 million shoes a year. Robots help the company produce new designs quickly.

Food Service Robots

Robots are decorating cakes and cupcakes in the bakery industry. Unifiller's Deco-Bot finishes cupcakes with twisted or rose-topped frosting in up to two colors. Deco-Bot can also be used to create custom cakes. A human operator designs a pattern and message on a touch screen tablet, and Deco-Bot creates it on a cake.

Deco-Bot

A designer creates a decorative pattern.

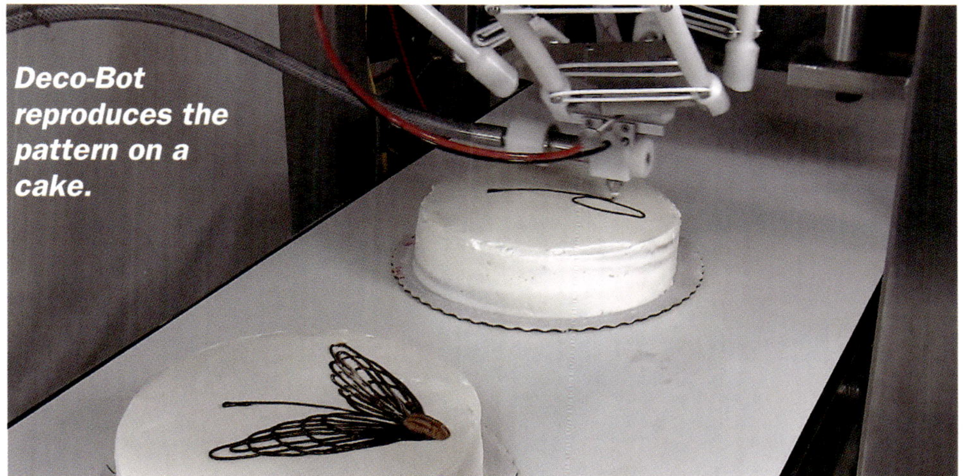

Deco-Bot reproduces the pattern on a cake.

Deco-Bot can write words and messages.

California's Creator restaurant has a 14-foot (4.3-m) -long burger-building robot. It uses 20 computers to cook and assemble hamburgers. Customers place an order at the start. While the burger is cooking, a bun travels down a chute and is sliced. The robot adds the customer's choice of  pickles, tomatoes, onions, lettuce, and cheese. The grilled meat is added last. Humans assist customers and stock the machine, but the cooking and assembly is done by robot.

Buns roll across the Creator restaurant's machine and drop down one-by-one to be sliced and placed in the customer's container.

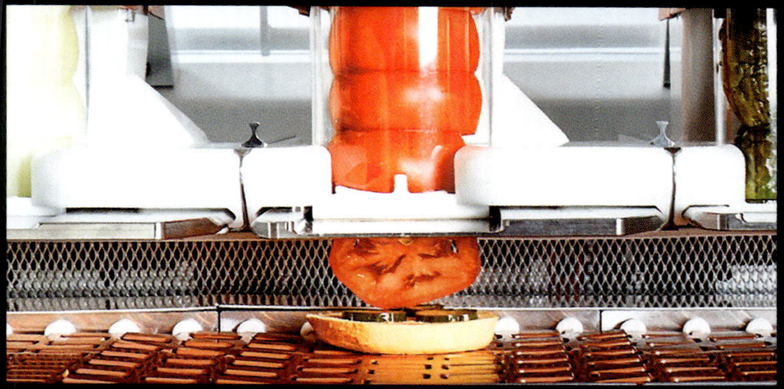

The customer's choice of "extras," such as tomatoes, are sliced and placed on the bun.

The finished burger comes out last, hot and ready to eat.

Zume Pizza of California uses a team of robot pizza makers to cook 200 pizzas per day. All of the ABB robots have names and specific jobs. John and Pepe place sauce on the dough. Marta spreads it evenly over the pie's surface. Bruno slides it into the oven. Vincenzo takes pizzas out of the hot oven and puts them on racks. These robots save staff members from some of the repetitive food production tasks, as well as protect them from hot ovens.

Marta spreads the sauce on a pizza.

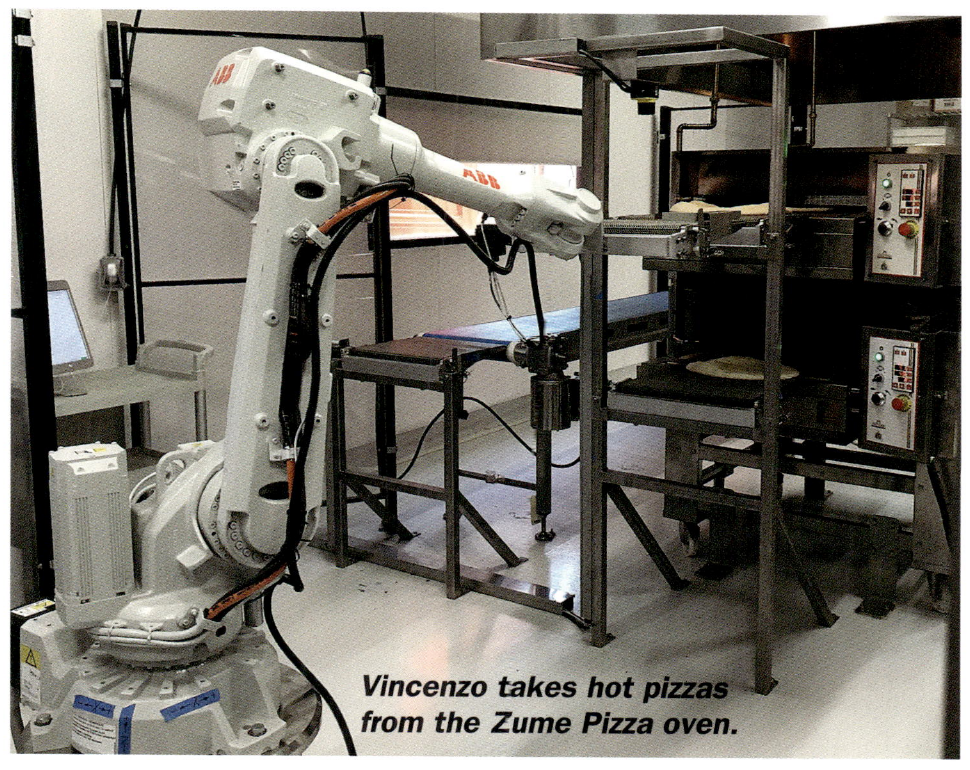

Vincenzo takes hot pizzas from the Zume Pizza oven.

Toy Industry Robots

Companies in the toy industry use millions of parts. They must fit exactly. Robots are the perfect workers for molding, building, and packaging toys. For example, a Lego factory may use as many as

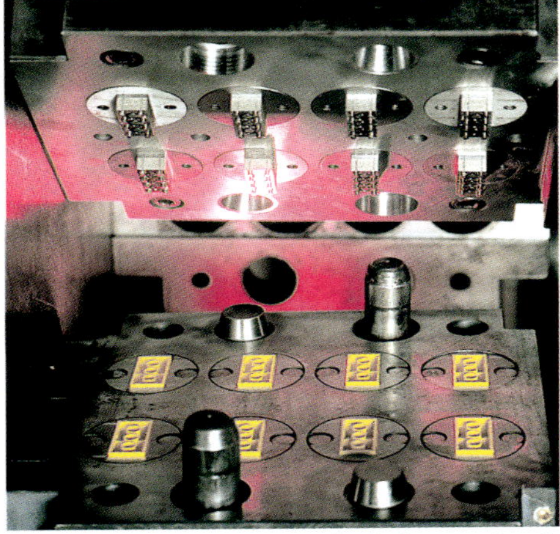

Robots mold Lego bricks out of hot plastic and then cool them down in less than 10 seconds.

1,000 robots. Some robots create Lego bricks and pieces. Robots take tiny arms, legs, hands, and heads to make the plastic characters. Other robots paint faces and details on Legos. Finally, packaging robots put the pieces into sets, and then into boxes. Robots help Lego keep up with the demand for billions of sets every year.

Up to 1,000 robots, and hundreds of human supervisors, may work in a Lego factory to keep up with demand for one of the world's most popular toys.

Warehouse Robots

Many robots work in warehouses. For companies that mail packages of products to customers, robots perform pick-pack-ship tasks. One robot takes an order and picks out the products from the warehouse. Another packages the products in boxes. A third robot creates the label with the customer's address. For companies such as Amazon, robots with human supervisors can work quickly and efficiently.

A Kuka industrial robot
shows how it can pick
a product from a large
number of choices.

A packing robot takes products that are ready to go
to customers, places the items in shipping boxes, and
tapes the packages shut. It can lift heavy products
and packages easily. This prevents injuries to humans.
Robot movements are fast and precise, helping
shipments move out of warehouses quickly.

*An ABB packing robot tapes
shut boxes of Lego toys.*

Warehouses use robots to move and store heavy boxes of goods. Boston Dynamics has created Handle to help. It is a mobile robot with both legs and wheels. The legs allow it to pick up heavy loads. The wheels let it move quickly up and down narrow aisles and throughout a warehouse. A human operator directs Handle with a remote control.

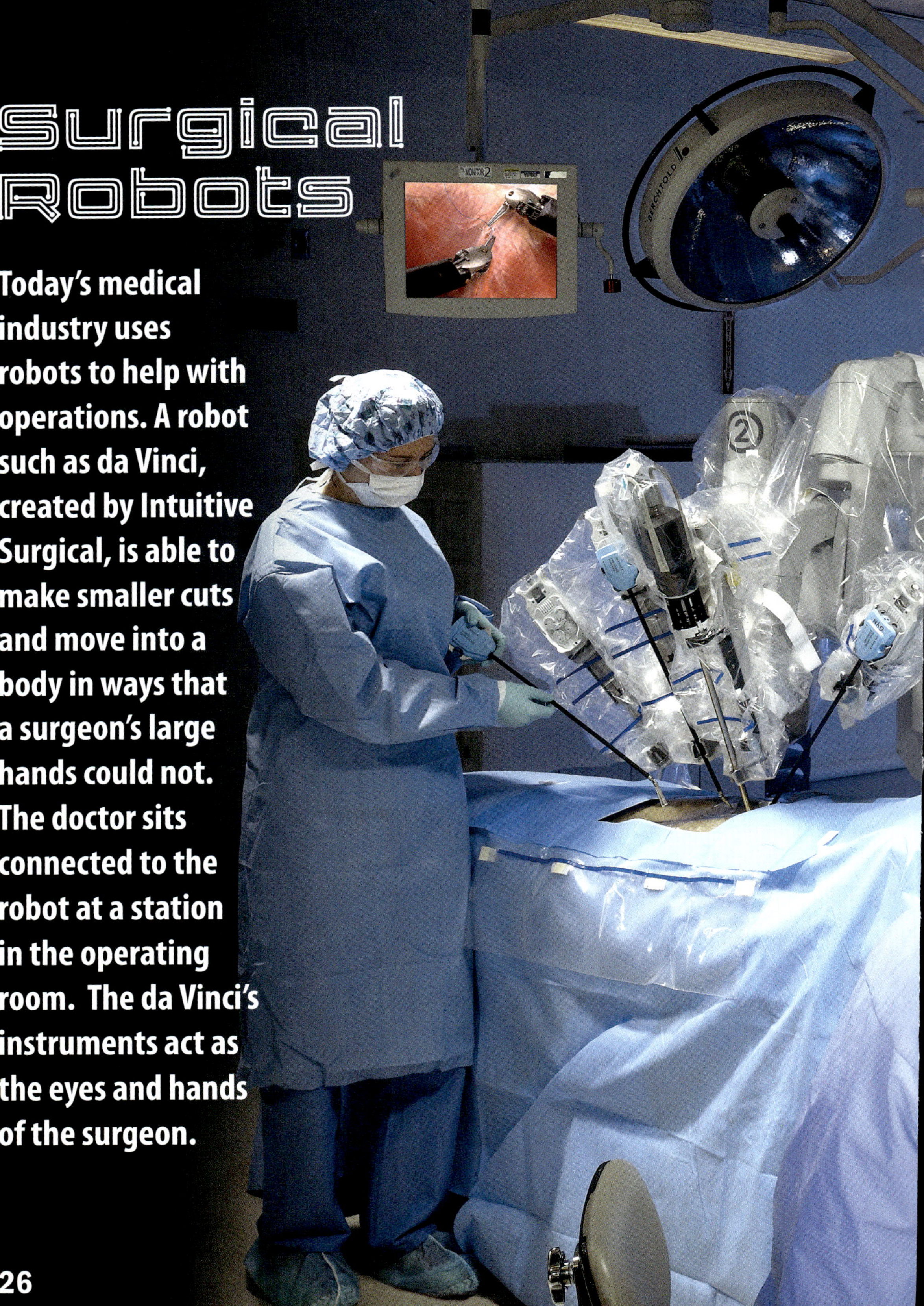

Surgical Robots

Today's medical industry uses robots to help with operations. A robot such as da Vinci, created by Intuitive Surgical, is able to make smaller cuts and move into a body in ways that a surgeon's large hands could not. The doctor sits connected to the robot at a station in the operating room. The da Vinci's instruments act as the eyes and hands of the surgeon.

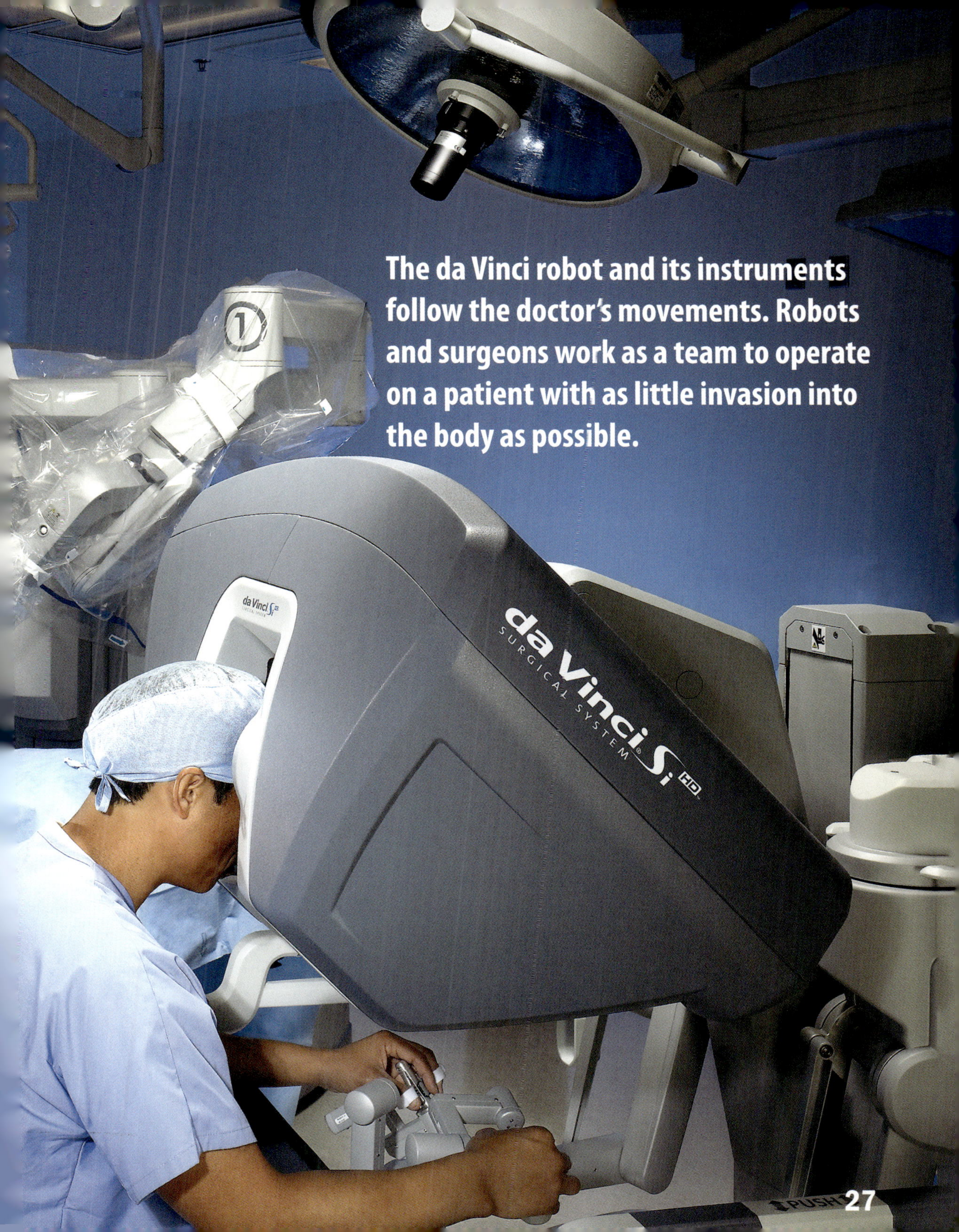

The da Vinci robot and its instruments follow the doctor's movements. Robots and surgeons work as a team to operate on a patient with as little invasion into the body as possible.

Cobot Robots

Many of today's mechanical workers are "cobot" robots. Cobot stands for "collaborative robot." Collaborative means that two or more humans and robots work together. Rethink Robotics created two cobot robots named Baxter and Sawyer. These robots are "taught" to do specific tasks in different industries. They can work in warehouses and manufacturing facilities. When extra hands are needed, cobot robots can be put to work.

Baxter was introduced as a cobot robot in 2012. Sawyer, a smaller, faster, and stronger robot, with one long arm, was developed in 2015.

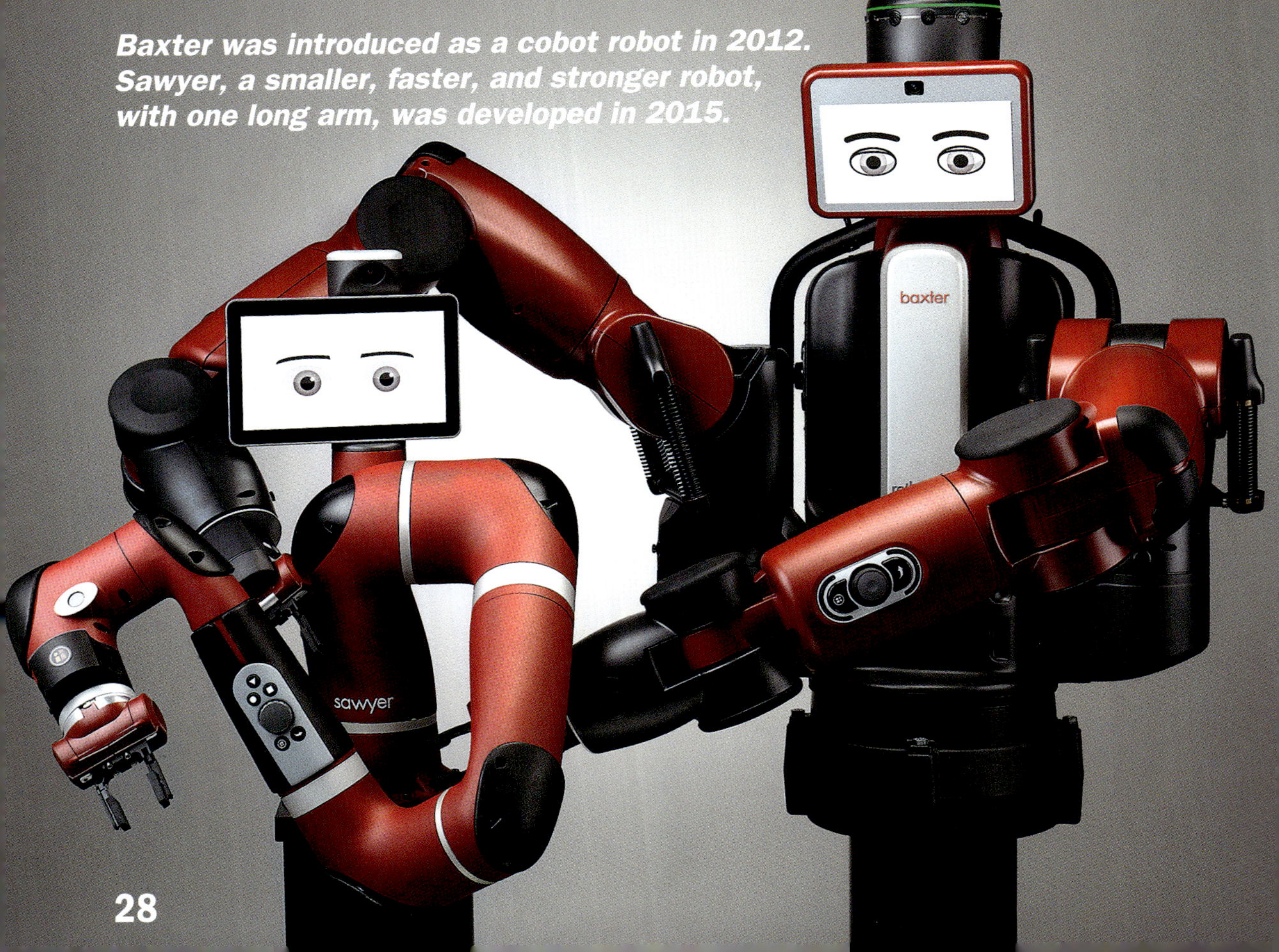

Cobot robots Baxter and Sawyer work closely with employees in a variety of jobs. Their human names and friendly faces make it easier for people to work with them.

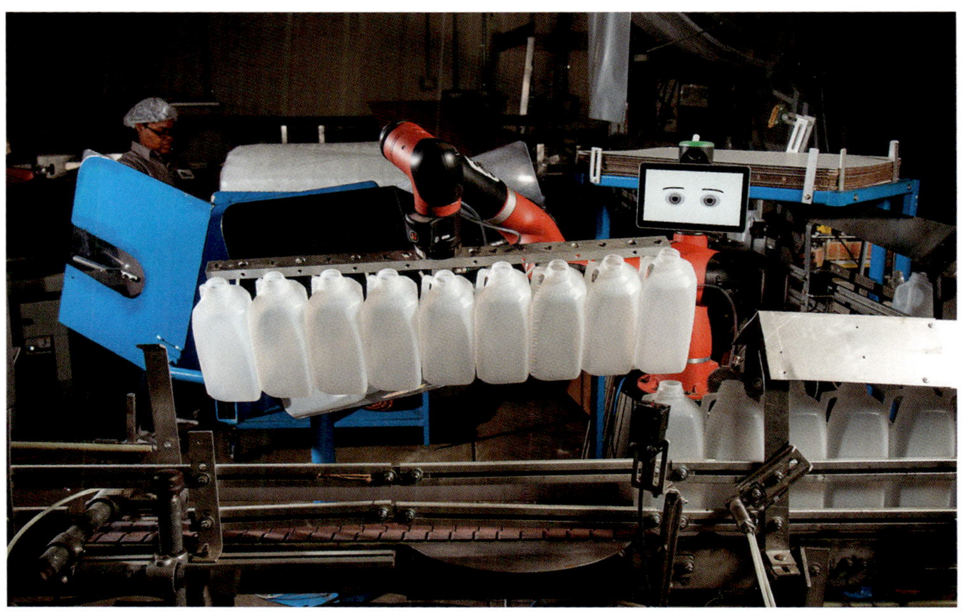

Glossary

ABB
A company based in Switzerland that produces many types of industrial robots.

Adhesive
A type of glue that sticks two objects together.

Assembly Line
A way of manufacturing goods in which parts are added to a semi-finished product as it moves from station to station. Many workers are used to make the product, but each worker is responsible for just one part or section. Assembly line goods can be made rapidly and efficiently.

Engineer
A person whose job is to use scientific knowledge to create and maintain mechanical and electronic objects and structures. This includes such things as robots, cameras, and engines.

Precise
Being exact and accurate. Robot workers are good at precise tasks.

PRIMER
A liquid used to coat a wood, metal, or canvas surface that helps paint stick to the object better.

REPETITIVE
Something that is done the same way over and over again.

RIVET
A short metal pin that is used to hold two pieces of metal, such as parts of a plane, together. The end of the rivet is pressed down to make a smooth surface.

WELD
To join two pieces of metal by heating them to the melting point and then pressing or hammering them together.

Online Resources

Booklinks
NONFICTION NETWORK
FREE! ONLINE NONFICTION RESOURCES

To learn more about industrial robots, visit abdobooklinks.com. These links are routinely monitored and updated to provide the most current information available.

Index

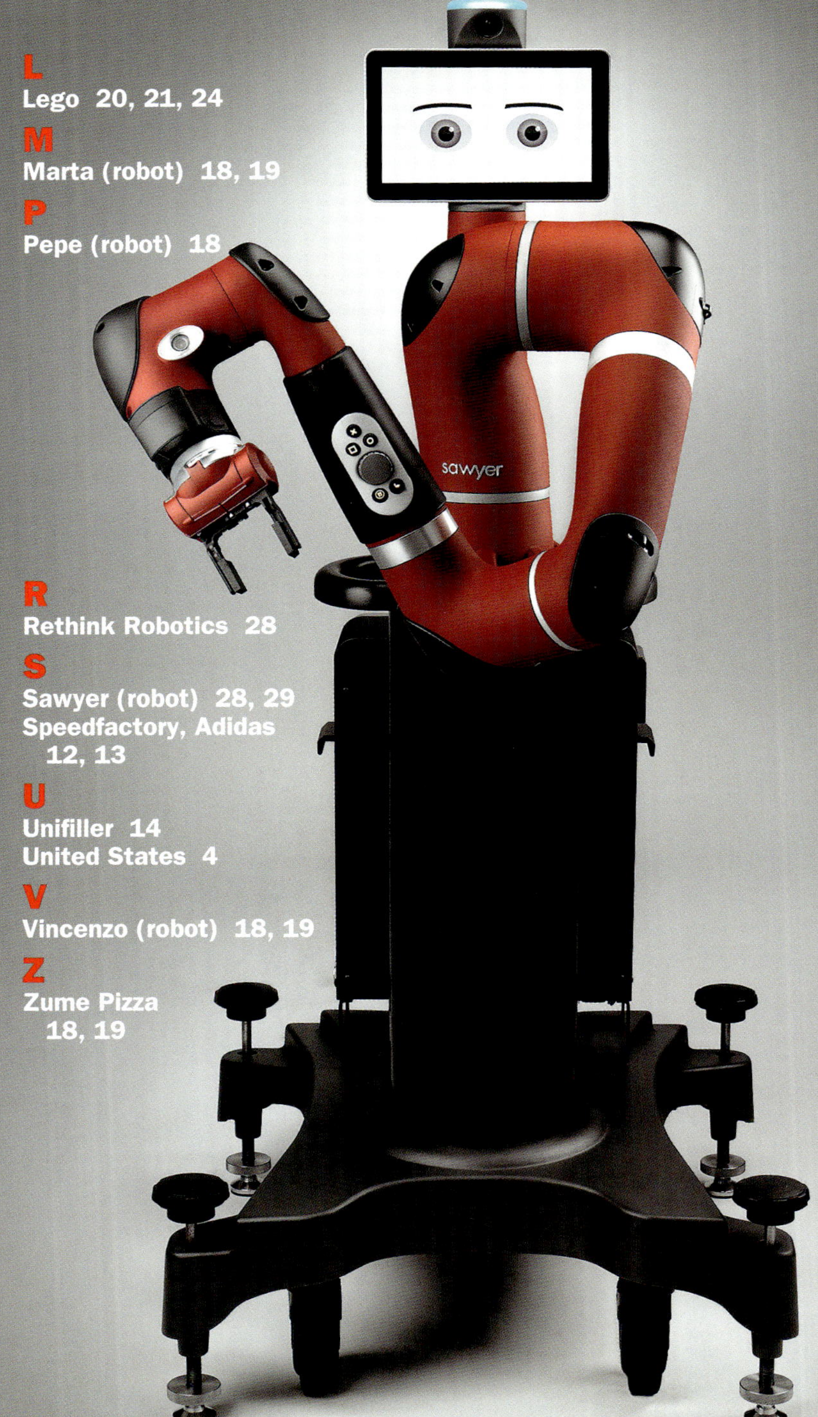